225	220	210	200	190	180	170	160	150

O R N I T H I S C H I A

Camptosaurus

Stegosaurus

MESOZOIC

TRIASSIC   JURASSIC

MILLIONS OF YEARS AGO

225	220	210	200	190	180	170	160	150

S A U R I S C H I A

Ornitholestes

Plateosaurus

"Ultrasaurus"
Allosaurus
Apatosaurus
Diplodocus
Megalosaurus
Brachiosaurus
"Supersaurus"

| 140 | 130 | 120 | 110 | 100 | 90 | 80 | 70 | 64 |

Hypsilophodon

Iguanodon

Hylaeosaurus

Anatosaurus

Parasaurolophus

Saurolophus

Corythosaurus

Lambeosaurus

Protoceratops

Psittacosaurus

Triceratops

Torosaurus

Ankylosaurus

Pentaceratops

Monoclonius

Maiasaura

CRETACEOUS

| 140 | 130 | 120 | 110 | 100 | 90 | 80 | 70 | 64 |

Deinonychus

Struthiomimus

Gallimimus

Daspletosaurus

Tyrannosaurus

Ornithomimus

Hypselosaurus

Stenonychosaurus

Gorgosaurus

Pterosaur

Dragonfly

Triceratops

Deinonychus

Stegosaurus

Coelophysis

Mammal

Procompsognathus

Frog

Dinosaurs

Apatosaurus

Allosaurus

Parasaurolophus

Archaeopteryx

Plateosaurus

Ankylosaurus

Turtle

Dinosaurs

By Daniel Cohen
Illustrated by
Jean Zallinger

DELL · YEARLING NONFICTION

YEARLING BOOKS/YOUNG YEARLINGS/YEARLING CLAS-SICS are designed especially to entertain and enlighten young people. Patricia Reilly Giff, consultant to this series, received her bachelor's degree from Marymount College and a master's degree in history from St. John's University. She holds a Professional Diploma in Reading and a Doctorate of Humane Letters from Hofstra University. She was a teacher and reading consultant for many years, and is the author of numerous books for young readers.

For a complete listing of all Yearling titles, write to
Dell Readers Service,
P.O. Box 1045,
South Holland, IL 60473.

To Mariah Wilson

Published by
Dell Publishing
a division of
Bantam Doubleday Dell Publishing Group, Inc.
666 Fifth Avenue
New York, New York 10103

Special thanks to Dr. Eugene Gaffney of the Department of Vertebrate Paleontology, American Museum of Natural History, for his careful review of the manuscript and illustrations.

ISBN: 0-440-40784-2

Reprinted by arrangement with Doubleday Books for Young Readers

Printed in the United States of America
May 1993
10 9 8 7 6 5 4 3 2 1
RAN

Compsognathus

Monoclonius

Masters of the World

Dinosaur is the name we give a large group of animals that dominated the earth millions of years ago. The word means "terrible lizard." It's a bit misleading. Dinosaurs aren't lizards, and many of them probably weren't very terrible. But the name has stuck.

All dinosaurs lived on the land. Most were very big—some were as long as ten cars, could have looked over the top of a four-story building, and weighed as much as a dozen elephants. There were small dinosaurs as well, some no bigger than a chicken.

Dinosaurs came in a great variety of fantastic shapes. Some had saber-like teeth and 6-inch-long claws. Other dinosaurs had 3-foot horns, armor plates, and spiked tails to protect themselves from the teeth and claws of their enemies. Some dinosaurs had crests, helmets, frills, and even duck-like bills.

The dinosaurs ran (often on two legs), jumped, stomped, waddled, and crawled across the earth's surface for over 140 million years. They were the most powerful animals of their time and were truly masters of the world.

How Do We Know About Them?

It's amazing to realize that a little more than one hundred and fifty years ago people had no idea that dinosaurs had ever existed. From time to time people had found dinosaur bones, but no one knew what they were or paid much attention to them.

Then in the 1820s and '30s scientists, mainly in England, began collecting some of these bones and teeth. As they studied the remains they realized that they had come from gigantic animals that had lived and died a long time ago. The British zoologist Sir Richard Owen invented the name "dinosaur" in 1841. Owen knew that the dinosaurs weren't just big lizards. He thought they resembled lizards in some ways but were really not like any living animal.

Ten years later, Owen helped build the first life-sized dinosaur models for a big exhibition in London. Though the models were all wrong, the people at the exhibition were amazed and astonished by these huge and strange-looking beasts. What they didn't know was that the real dinosaurs were far larger and stranger-looking than the models.

What Are Fossils?

We have learned about dinosaurs through studying fossils—the remains of any ancient plant or animal. Dinosaur fossils are either bones, skin imprints, or footprints. Most of the dinosaurs that existed never became fossils. But at a few places in the world conditions were just right, and large numbers of dinosaur fossils have been found.

Scientists who specialize in studying fossils are called "paleontologists" (pay-lee-on-TOL-o-gists). Sometimes they find whole skeletons. More often the bones are scattered. The paleontologists then have to try to reconstruct what the animal was like when it was alive.

The bones of a dinosaur can give us a pretty good idea of what it looked like. But there are things that bones cannot tell us. For example, we don't know what color dinosaurs were and we don't know how they acted.

There are new finds of dinosaur fossils all the time, and old evidence is given new interpretations. So while the dinosaurs have been dead for millions of years, our ideas about them are still changing.

The World of the Dinosaurs

Two hundred and fifty million years ago, when the first dinosaurs began to evolve, the earth looked very different from the way it looks today. There were no separate continents. All the land was clumped together in one gigantic supercontinent. As the ages passed, this great land mass broke apart, and the large chunks of land that we now call continents slowly drifted away from one another.

The Age of Dinosaurs lasted about 140 million years, and the earth changed greatly over that immense period of time. In general, the world was warmer and flatter than it is today. There were fewer mountains and more swamps and shallow seas.

Dinosaurs were not the only creatures on earth. As the dinosaurs were beginning to emerge, so too were the first mammals. The most common ones were tiny and resembled modern shrews. Many of the animals that lived alongside the dinosaurs are still alive today. Frogs, turtles and crocodiles, and many types of insects were common. Fully modern birds appeared late in the Mesozoic. And the lowly, slow-moving opossum was as much at home in the dinosaur's world as it is in our suburbs.

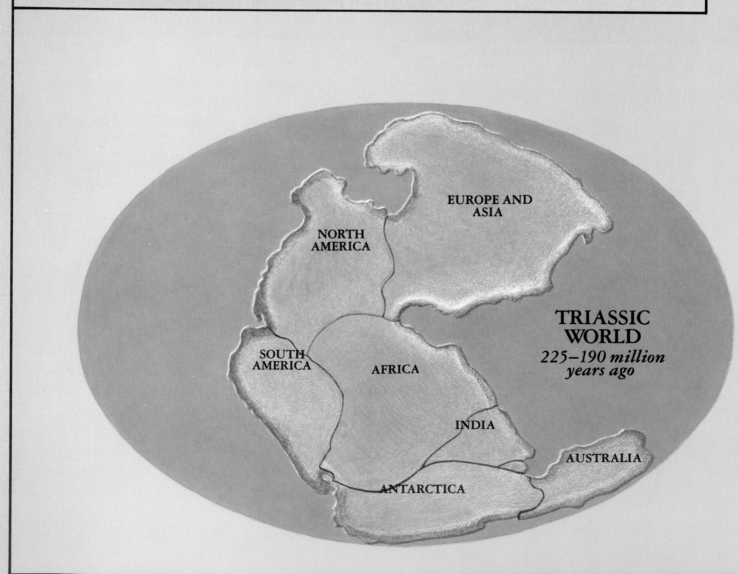

EUROPE AND ASIA

NORTH AMERICA

SOUTH AMERICA

AFRICA

INDIA

AUSTRALIA

ANTARCTICA

TRIASSIC WORLD
225–190 million years ago

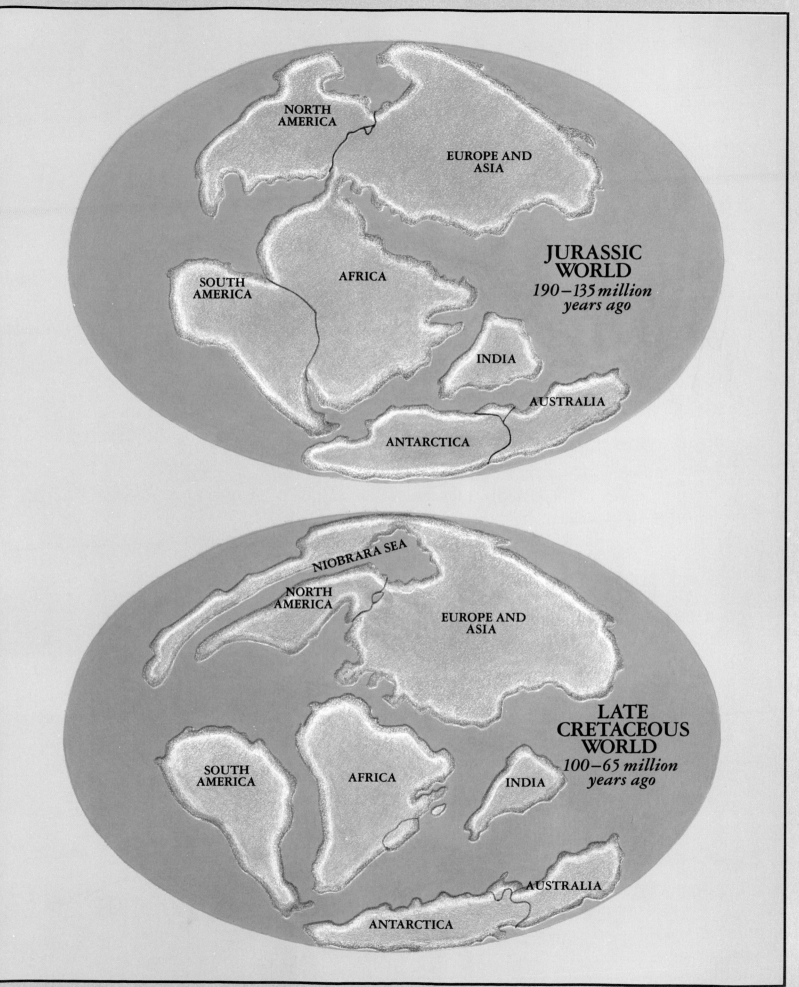

JURASSIC WORLD
190—135 million years ago

NORTH AMERICA

EUROPE AND ASIA

SOUTH AMERICA

AFRICA

INDIA

AUSTRALIA

ANTARCTICA

LATE CRETACEOUS WORLD
100—65 million years ago

NIOBRARA SEA

NORTH AMERICA

EUROPE AND ASIA

SOUTH AMERICA

AFRICA

INDIA

AUSTRALIA

ANTARCTICA

TRIASSIC ERA   225 – 190 million years ago

JURASSIC ERA   190 – 135 million years ago

When Did They Live?

It's often said that dinosaurs lived "when the earth was young." That's not really true. The periods of time we must deal with are so huge, they are difficult to grasp.

According to the best estimates, the earth was formed 4,600 *million* years ago. The simplest form of life didn't appear for over another 1,000 *million* years, and the first dinosaurs evolved a mere 250 million years ago.

Think of it this way: if the entire history of the earth could be reduced to a single twenty-four-hour period, then the dinosaurs would be seen less than an hour before the day was over. In that day the whole history of human civilization would take about half a second!

Scientists divide the history of the earth into what they call geologic time periods. The dinosaurs lived mainly during the era called Mesozoic (mez-oh-ZO-ic), the age of "middle life." The Mesozoic is further divided into three periods, each of which had its own type of dinosaurs. They are the Triassic (try-ASS-ic), about 225 to 190 million years ago, the Jurassic (joo-RASS-ic), about 190 to 135 million years ago, and the Cretaceous (creh-TAY-shus), about 135 to 65 million years ago.

CRETACEOUS ERA   135 – 65 million years ago

Different Kinds of Dinosaurs

Scientists classify dinosaurs into two main groups or orders, not on the basis of size or shape, but because of the type of hipbones they have. One of the major orders is called the Saurischia (sawr-ISS-kee-a) or "lizard-hipped." The other is called the Ornithischia (orn-i-THISS-kee-a) or "bird-hipped."

It's easy to remember which kind of dinosaur belongs to each order. The saurischians include two of the best-known dinosaurs—the gigantic long-necked, small-headed plant eaters like *Brontosaurus* (bront-o-SAW-rus) and the short-necked, big-headed, two-legged meat eaters like *Tyrannosaurus* (tie-RAN-oh-SAW-rus). The smaller relatives of both kinds are also saurischians.

Practically all other kinds of dinosaurs are ornithischians. That includes the duck-billed dinosaurs, the armored dinosaurs, the horned dinosaurs and the rest.

The saurischians appear closer to the ancestral reptiles. The ornithischians branched off very early in dinosaur history, and the first forms appear to have been two-legged. Later, a number of species returned to a four-legged posture.

Ornithischian Bird-hipped

Monoclonius

Allosaurus

Saurischian Lizard-hipped

(Brontosaurus)
Apatosaurus

How Many Kinds?

How many different species of dinosaurs were there? It's not an easy question to answer.

When scientists classify dinosaurs, they try to figure out how closely they are related to one another. First they put them in one of the two orders, Saurischia or Ornithischia. Then they work down to suborders, family, genus, and species. The species is the smallest unit of classification. Species and genus names are written in italics.

Sometimes there is a great confusion of names, with the same dinosaur being given more than one name. One of the best-known dinosaurs, *Brontosaurus,* is the subject of just such confusion. The name, which means "thunder lizard," was given to the creature by the paleontologist Edward Drinker Cope at the end of the last century.

However, remains of the very same dinosaur had been discovered earlier by Cope's deadly rival in fossil hunting, Othniel Charles Marsh. Marsh called the creature *Apatosaurus* (a-PAT-oh-SAW-rus). Today most scientists call the dinosaur *Apatosaurus,* because the honor of naming an animal goes to the person who discovered it. But the name *Brontosaurus* has been popular for years, and that's the name most of us know.

New types of dinosaur are turning up all the time. Over fifty new species have been discovered since 1970. The best guess is that we have discovered about 300 different species of dinosaur.

Were They Reptiles?

From the time dinosaurs were discovered, scientists assumed that they were reptiles. That is, they were most closely related to modern lizards and crocodiles. Even today most scientists still say that dinosaurs were reptiles. But some have started to question that belief. They say that dinosaurs were—well, simply dinosaurs, in a class all by themselves.

Reptiles lay eggs. We know that some dinosaurs did. Reptiles have scales. A few fossils have had enough preserved skin to indicate that some dinosaurs also had scales. Reptiles are cold-blooded. Were dinosaurs? There is a big question about that.

Diplodocus

To say an animal is cold-blooded doesn't mean that the animal's blood is always cold. It means the animal doesn't have any internal temperature controls. Lizards and crocodiles are cold-blooded. Birds, dogs, and people are warm-blooded. Your temperature remains about the same on a cold day as it is on a warm day. But when the air temperature drops, so does the internal temperature of a lizard or crocodile. They get sluggish. If they get too cold they die. To warm up, reptiles must sit in the sun. Warm-blooded animals can be more active. But they must also eat more to maintain their temperature.

Some scientists now think that dinosaurs were built more like fast-moving, warm-blooded animals than like sluggish reptiles. Even those scientists who still class dinosaurs as reptiles say they were a very special kind of reptile.

The Not-so-dumb Dinosaurs

Most dinosaurs had big bodies and tiny brains. *Diplodocus* (di-PLOD-uh-kus) was ninety feet long and had a brain the size of a small potato. It's amazing that a brain that small could control such a huge body.

But not all dinosaurs were stupid giants. In 1968 the remains of a dinosaur called *Stenonychosaurus* (sten-ON-ik-uh-SAW-rus) were found in Canada. It was small for a dinosaur, about 6 feet from nose to tail, and lightly built. It was a meat eater that ran down its prey on long slender legs and grabbed it with well-developed hands. It had sharp vision and a good sense of smell.

What really fascinated scientists about *Stenonychosaurus* was the size of its brain. The dinosaur was as big as an ostrich, and its brain was the size of an ostrich's brain. Most scientists think that *Stenonychosaurus* was the smartest dinosaur yet discovered. He certainly wasn't the near brainless mountain of flesh that people usually think of when they hear the word "dinosaur."

Stenonychosaurus

Gallimimus

The Speedy Dinosaur

Most modern reptiles, crocodiles, lizards, and turtles are sprawlers. Their legs are set wide apart so they can flop down when they get tired. Dinosaurs were not built that way. The dinosaurs that ran on four legs had their legs tucked beneath them like horses or elephants. The big horned dinosaurs like *Triceratops* (try-SAIR-a-tops) could probably gallop along at speeds up to 30 miles per hour.

A lot of dinosaurs, including the big carnivores or meat eaters like *Tyrannosaurus,* stood on their two powerful hind legs. In order to catch their fleeing prey, they had to be able to run at least as fast. *Tyrannosaurus* and others like him thundered along with their bodies bent forward, tail held out stiffly behind.

The real speedsters of the dinosaur world were the smaller dinosaurs. The thirteen-foot-long *Gallimimus* (GAL-ih-MIME-us) was probably the best runner. This beaked, bird-like creature might have hit 60 miles per hour, making it one of the fastest animals that ever lived.

Dinosaur Eggs

Dinosaurs—at least most of them—laid eggs. In 1922 an American expedition in Mongolia found nests of eggs of *Protoceratops* (pro-toe-SAIR-a-tops). An adult dinosaur of this type was about 6 feet long. The eggs, which were rather sausage-shaped, were 8 inches long. That's larger than a chicken egg, which is about 2 inches. But *Protoceratops* grew to be a lot larger than any chicken.

The biggest known dinosaur egg belonged to *Hypselosaurus* (HIP-see-loh-SAW-rus). The dinosaur, a medium-sized relative of the *Brontosaurus,* grew to a length of 40 feet. Its eggs, however, were only a foot long.

How about the really big dinosaurs like *Brachiosaurus* (BRACK-ee-oh-SAW-rus), which was twice the size of *Hypselosaurus.* Did they lay eggs that were 2 feet long? We have never found a *Brachiosaurus* egg, but it's safe to say the eggs were nowhere near that size. The bigger the egg, the thicker the shell that is needed to contain it. A 2-foot egg would need a shell so thick that a baby dinosaur would not be able to break it and get out.

Some scientists have speculated that the really large dinosaurs did not lay eggs at all, but bore their young alive.

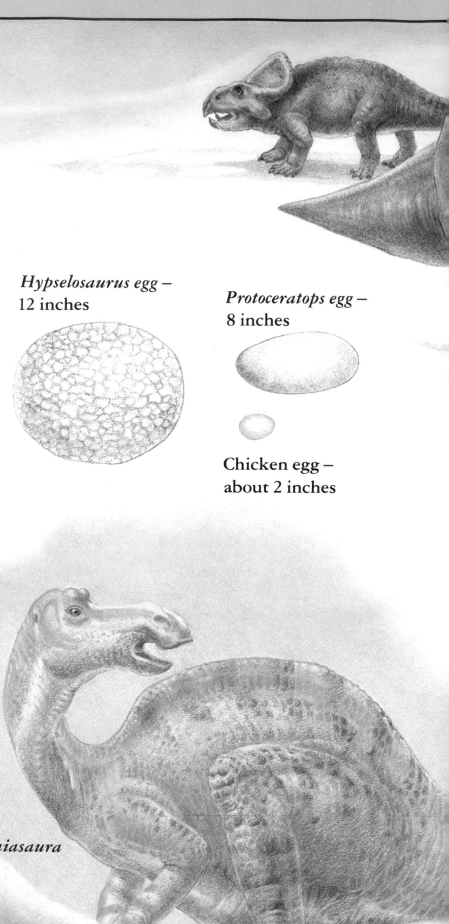

Hypselosaurus egg — 12 inches

Protoceratops egg — 8 inches

Chicken egg — about 2 inches

Maiasaura

Part of a fossilized *Protoceratops* nest in Field Museum in Chicago

Protoceratops

2 ft.

Based on Jay Makela's find on Egg Mountain, Montana – probably *hypsilophodont*

Dinosaur Family Life

Modern reptiles bury their eggs in the ground and crawl away. The eggs are hatched by the heat of the sun, and the young must fend for themselves as soon as they are hatched. Dinosaurs were much more careful.

In 1978 and 1979 a new type of dinosaur was discovered in Montana. Not only were adult skeletons found, there were also skeletons of baby dinosaurs, and nests of the dinosaur's eggs, all in the same area. The adults were 30 feet long. The babies were 3½ feet long. They were young but they were too big to have been just hatched.

The nests were mounds of earth about 7 feet across. The eggs had been arranged in layers. In each layer the elongated eggs had been carefully placed in a circle, like the spokes of a wheel. Every layer was covered with sand, and then the entire nest was covered.

Both adult and young—but not newly hatched—dinosaurs were found nearby, indicating that the family might have stayed around the nest. Perhaps the full-grown dinosaurs helped protect the eggs? Several nests were found in the area, which seemed to suggest that the family came back to the same place year after year.

Scientists gave this new dinosaur the name *Maiasaura* (MY-a-SAW-ra) which means "good mother reptile."

Maiasaura

Triceratops

A Herd of Dinosaurs

Many dinosaurs, it seems, were sociable creatures. Fossil footprints show a large number of the same type of dinosaur moving in the same direction at the same time.

In Africa today, large plant-eating animals gather in enormous herds and travel long distances in search of food. It's possible that large plant-eating dinosaurs like *Iguanodon* (ig-WAH-no-don) and *Triceratops* did the same. The young dinosaurs might have traveled in the middle of the herd for protection. Even the largest and hungriest

Tyrannosaurus would hesitate to attack a full-grown *Triceratops,* much less a whole herd of them. There is evidence that the gigantic *Brontosaurus* also traveled in herds. The sight would have been awesome—giants tramping through the forests, stripping trees of their leaves and fruit in their endless search for food.

The young, the size of full-grown elephants, would be in the center of the herd. Ringing the group would be weathered 70-foot-long bulls, waving their necks to catch the scent of fresh food, or of a nearby predator.

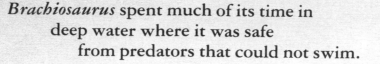

Brachiosaurus spent much of its time in deep water where it was safe from predators that could not swim.

The Biggest Dinosaur

For a long time the biggest known dinosaur was *Brachiosaurus* (BRACK-ee-oh-SAW-rus). This giant stood on four powerful legs, and had a heavy body, a huge neck, and a very small head. He could look over the top of a four-story building and he weighed 80 tons. *Brachiosaurus* probably used his great height to clip leaves from the tops of trees. He could get at food that smaller plant eaters couldn't reach.

Then in 1971 parts of the skeleton of a dinosaur like *Brachiosaurus,* but even bigger, were found in Colorado. This creature could look over the top of a five-story building and might have weighed 100 tons. It was nicknamed "Supersaurus."

That wasn't the end. In 1979 the bones of another gigantic creature were once again found in Colorado. This one may have been able to look into a sixth-story window and could have weighed 140 tons. This new dinosaur was nicknamed "Ultrasaurus."

Without more complete skeletons there is a lot about Supersaurus and Ultrasaurus that we still don't know. And were they really the biggest dinosaurs, or just the biggest that we have found so far?

How Did the Giants Eat?

All the really gigantic dinosaurs like *Brachiosaurus* and the familiar *Brontosaurus* belong to the group called Sauropoda (SAWR-oh-POD-a). They all had the same general shape—large, heavy bodies, long tails and necks, and tiny heads. And they were all plant eaters. Scientists are not sure how these giants got enough to eat.

The teeth of the sauropods are small and relatively weak, not at all like the huge grinding molars that elephants use to chew up plants. The sauropods and other plant eaters must have swallowed vast quantities of vegetation whole. They may also have swallowed stones, to help grind up the food once it was in their stomach. Chickens and other birds swallow grit for that purpose.

We can't be sure how much food these giants needed. A *Brontosaurus* weighed 30 or 40 tons—ten times as much as a 3- or 4-ton elephant. If it needed ten times as much food, then it would have to eat half a ton of vegetation each day. It's difficult to imagine how it could have gotten that much food through its little mouth. Most scientists, however, assume that the *Brontosaurus* and other sauropods did not require nearly as much food per pound as an elephant. Still, the life of these giants must have been a constant search for enough to eat.

The elephant, the largest living land animal, would have looked tiny next to a *Brontosaurus*.

Being a Giant

The largest land animal in the modern world is the elephant. Most dinosaurs were bigger than elephants, and some were many times the size of an elephant.

Being a giant had some advantages. The great sauropods could reach the leaves at the tops of trees. Peaceful giants were safe from enemies unless they were attacked by equally gigantic predators. There was plenty of vegetation in the Mesozoic world and plenty of meat as well.

At one time some scientists believed that the great sauropods were so heavy that they could never come out of the water, which would have helped support their massive bodies. But study of sauropod tracks shows that they could walk, and possibly run quite effectively, on dry land. However, these giants probably did spend part of their time in water.

The nostrils of most sauropods are high on the skull. In that giant of giants, *Brachiosaurus,* the nostrils actually stick up above the skull roof. So it's reasonable to believe that these giants often waded in deep water in search of water plants to eat. With just the tops of their heads breaking the surface, they could breathe and look out for danger.

Brachiosaurus

Tyrannosaurus

Allosaurus

Gorgosaurus

26

Daspletosaurus

The "Tyrant" and His Family

The *Tyrannosaurus* was the largest of the carnivorous dinosaurs. In fact, it was the largest carnivorous animal of any kind ever to walk the earth.

Tyrannosaurus appeared fairly late in the dinosaurs' long history. It was the descendant of a long line of fearsome killers like *Allosaurus* (AL-uh-SAW-rus) and *Megalosaurus* (MEG-a-low-SAW-rus). During the time *Tyrannosaurus* lived, there were other big carnivores like *Gorgosaurus* (gor-go-SAW-rus) and *Daspletosaurus* (dass-PLEE-toh-SAW-rus). They all had outsized heads and great gaping mouths lined with dagger-like teeth. They all walked about on strong hind legs. Their front legs were small and the claws were used for grasping prey. Any one of them could have swallowed a person whole, if there had

been any people around to swallow.

But the *Tyrannosaurus* was the biggest on its family tree—a monster among monsters. It was 50 feet from tail to nose, and stood almost 20 feet from the ground to the top of its head. It must have weighed at least 8 tons.

Its skull alone was 4 feet long and the jaws, which stretched much of the length of the skull, possessed sharp, serrated 6-inch teeth.

It has been suggested that fierce *Tyrannosaurus* and his kin were mainly scavengers—that is, they ate dead animals because they didn't have the speed to catch live ones. They probably wouldn't pass up a meal, dead or alive. But these creatures were so well adapted to attacking and killing that most scientists are now sure these giants were the greatest hunters ever.

27

Hylaeosaurus

Ankylosaurus

The Armored Dinosaurs

In a world populated with giant killers like *Tyrannosaurus,* the plant-eating dinosaurs had to have ways of defending themselves. One way was to be so well armored that the predators couldn't or wouldn't attack.

One of the early armored dinosaurs, and also one of the first dinosaurs to be discovered was *Hylaeosaurus* (HY-lee-oh-SAW-rus). The back of this 20-foot dinosaur was covered by tough, bony plates. It was further protected by rows of spines that stuck out sideways along the creature's body, and upwards along the tail.

The largest and most completely armored of this group, *Ankylosaurus* (ang-kuh-lo-SAW-rus), appeared late in dinosaur history. This was the true tank of the dinosaur world. Its 32-foot length was entirely covered by heavy armored plates. Even the top of its skull was armored. These plates were spiked, and at the end of its tail *Ankylosaurus* had a massive bony club.

Ankylosaurus was a peaceful, slow-moving creature that spent much of its life grazing. To the unwary predator it would have looked like an easy meal. But when threatened, *Ankylosaurus* would crouch down so only its armor was exposed. If the predator tried to turn *Ankylosaurus* over, it would receive a shattering blow from the dinosaur's clubbed tail.

The Duck-billed Dinosaurs

Among the most common dinosaurs are the members of a large group called the hadrosaurs (HAD-ruh-sawrs), or duck-billed dinosaurs. They were large animals, averaging 30 or 40 feet from snout to tail and weighing 5 or 6 tons. Hadrosaurs were vegetarians that walked on their strong hind legs. They may have dropped down on all fours to run. In most hadrosaurs, the front end of the skull was long and broad and looked much like a gigantic duck bill.

The classic duck-billed dinosaur was *Anatosaurus* (a-NAT-oh-SAW-rus). This dinosaur probably used its broad snout for probing and shoveling for plants and roots in the mud on the bottom of lakes or streams.

Anatosaurus was a flat-headed hadrosaur. There was also a large group of crested hadrosaurs. The skulls of these creatures were adorned with an astonishing variety of bony crests, helmets, horns, and pillars. *Saurolophus* (sawr-OL-o-fus) had a crest of solid bone. It was probably used for display like the brightly colored feathers on many birds.

In other hadrosaurs the crests were hollow. *Corythosaurus* (ko-RITH-oh-SAW-rus) had a hollow, helmet-like crest that covered the entire top of its skull. *Parasaurolophus* (par-a-sawr-OL-oh-fus) had a remarkable long hollow tube that curved back over its shoulders.

These crests would have enabled the hadrosaurs to make a variety of distinctive and very loud honking and tooting noises. The hadrosaurs may have kept in touch with members of their herd by making such noises. Or they may have bellowed and honked at one another in a threat or display.

Anatosaurus

Saurolophus

Parasaurolophus

Corythosaurus

The Horned Dinosaurs

With its huge head lowered, three horns pointing forward, and with its body—weighing several tons—propelled on powerful legs, *Triceratops* would have been a match for anything. Add to this the possibility that *Triceratops* traveled in large herds, and you can assume that this dinosaur had little to fear.

Triceratops is the best known of a large group of ceratopsian (SAIR-a-TOP-see-an) or horned-face dinosaurs. They were all the same basic shape, with heavy bodies, huge horned heads, and a large bony frill at the back of the skull.

Ceratopsians could have a single horn on the snout like *Monoclonius* (MON-oh-KLO-nee-us) or five horns like *Pentaceratops* (PEN-ta-SAIR-a-tops). There was one on the snout, one above each eye, and one on each cheek. The horns of a ceratopsian could be long or short, straight or curved.

Frills came in various lengths. The frill of a ceratopsian could be solid or have holes in it, and it could be decorated with spikes, scallops, or knobs. The longest frill belonged to *Torosaurus* (tor-oh-SAW-rus). The skull measured 8 1/2 feet from the tip of the nose to the end of the frill. It had the biggest head of any known land animal. *Torosaurus* itself was only about 25 feet long.

Triceratops

Monoclonius

Torosaurus

"One of the Strangest of Animals"

The remains of *Stegosaurus* (STEG-oh-SAW-rus) were first discovered in 1877. When they were shown to the great British zoologist Richard Owen, he remarked that it was "one of the strangest of animals."

Today we know a lot more about *Stegosaurus* than Owen did, yet in many respects it's still a puzzle.

Stegosaurus was an average-sized dinosaur, reaching up to 30 feet in length, with a bulky body. Its head was almost ridiculously small, and its brain was about the size of a walnut. Near the base of the creature's spine was a large bundle of nerve tissue. This has led to the false impression that *Stegosaurus* had two brains, one in front and one in back. The well-developed nerve bundle may have helped the dinosaur control its back legs, but it wasn't a second brain.

Stegosaurus stood firmly on four feet; however, the front legs were so much shorter than the back legs that it looked oddly unbalanced.

The strangest feature of all was the row of large, triangular armored plates that ran down the middle of its back. Scientists have long believed that these plates ran in a double row, but a recent reconstruction of what *Stegosaurus* may have looked like shows the creature with a single row of plates. Two pair of wicked-looking spikes at the end of the creature's tail were used as a weapon against any predators that might get too close.

Stegosaurus

The "Terrible Claw"

In 1964 the well-preserved remains of a new type of carnivorous dinosaur were discovered in Montana. It wasn't particularly large—just about 8 feet from nose to tail. Like most other meat eaters it walked on two feet. Its small front legs were adapted for grasping and holding. It ran with its head up and its body parallel to the ground, holding its tail out stiffly behind for balance.

The most distinctive thing about the creature was its feet. It walked on two toes. The third curved upward as a wicked-looking 5-inch claw. The claw could only have been used for slashing and tearing food or foe. The creature was given the name *Deinonychus* (dine-ON-ik-us), or "terrible claw."

In life, *Deinonychus* must have run down its prey and grasped it in its front claws. Then, standing on one foot, it would slash the victim to death with the curved claw on the other foot.

Everything about *Deinonychus* suggests speed, agility, and ferocity.

Deinonychus

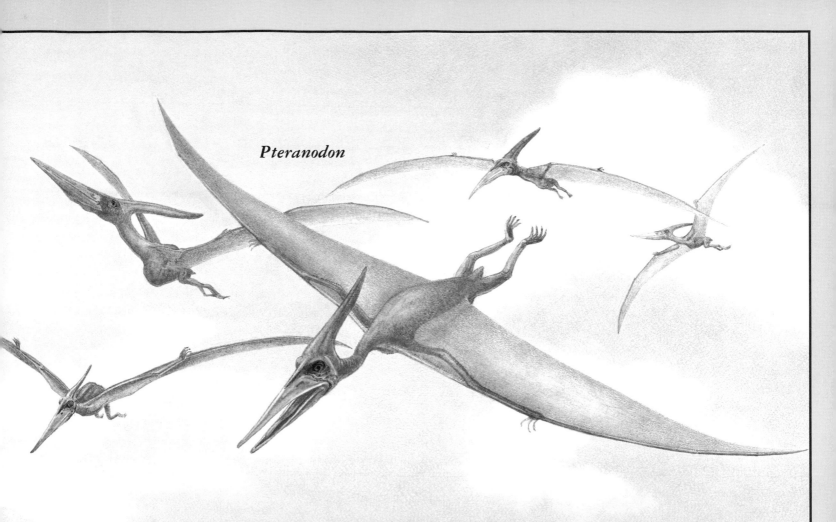

Pteranodon

Rulers of the Sky

While the dinosaurs walked the earth, the sky was dominated by pterosaurs (TAIR-a-sawrs). These winged creatures were not, as once thought, ancestors to the birds. Nor were they flying dinosaurs. They were a separate group.

Most pterosaurs were small, with long toothy jaws and, often, long tails. But the giants like *Pteranodon* (te-RAN-a-don) have always attracted the most attention. It had a 20-foot wingspan, a huge toothless beak, and an equally huge bony crest at the back of its skull. The body was relatively tiny.

To stay aloft, *Pteranodon* had to be extremely light. It's estimated that the creature weighed as little as 20 pounds.

Pteranodon was probably more of a glider than a flier, because it didn't have the muscles to flap its huge wings. It is not clear how *Pteranodon* was able to take off or land without breaking its fragile bones and tearing its paper-thin wings. Scientists agreed that *Pteranodon* was not only the largest flying creature that ever lived, it was the largest flying creature that *could* ever have lived. Anything larger would have been too heavy to fly.

Then in 1972 the partial remains of a pterosaur twice the size of *Pteranodon* were found. Until a complete skeleton is unearthed, we won't know what this giant of the air really looked like, but all the ideas about how big is too big to fly must be thrown out.

Ichthyosaurus

Elasmosaurus

Tylosaurus

Rulers of the Sea

The seas of the Mesozoic also contained a remarkable variety of huge and strange creatures. There were the ichthyosaurs (IK-the-a-sawrs) or "fish reptiles." The name is very appropriate because they really were shaped like fish, although they were reptiles. They also looked a lot like porpoises and dolphins, which are mammals. This is a perfect illustration of *adaptation:* how different types of animals—in this case fish, reptiles, and mammals—can develop similar qualities when faced with similar conditions.

Most ichthyosaurs were 10 or 15 feet in length, but fragmentary remains indicate that one type may have been over 50 feet long, which puts it in a class with modern whales.

The plesiosaurs (PLEE-zee-a-sawrs) didn't look at all like fish. Most of them had fat bodies, short tails, and enormous necks. They propelled themselves through the water by means of four paddle-like flippers. The 43-foot *Elasmosaurus* (ee-laz-mo-SAWR-us) had a neck that was as long as its body and tail combined.

A third type of sea dweller was the mosasaurs (MOZE-a-sawrs). They looked like the legendary sea serpent, with long, tapering bodies and large heads with pointed snouts and wicked-looking teeth. Some were 30 feet long; others may have been even larger.

The Feathered Dinosaur

In 1860 a most amazing fossil was discovered in Germany. The bones looked as if they belonged to a small dinosaur. However, the rocks had also preserved an impression of what covered it. The creature was quite clearly covered with feathers. It was named *Archaeopteryx* (ARK-kee-OP-ter-ix), which means "ancient feather."

Archaeopteryx was quickly labeled the "first bird." Yet there were some unbirdlike things about it. It had teeth, a long tail, and well-developed claws on its wings. Strangest of all, despite its wings and feathers it almost certainly couldn't fly well. It didn't have the flight muscles a bird needs. But it may have been able to climb a tree, jump off, and glide a short distance.

Archaeopteryx could have used its wings to trap the insects that made up most of its diet.

Recently some scientists have suggested that *Archaeopteryx* was really a small feathered dinosaur. They figure that if dinosaurs were warm-blooded—that is, if the creatures generated their own body heat—then they needed some covering to stop heat loss. Feathers are excellent insulators.

Archaeopteryx

Ostrich

Ornithomimus

Dinosaurs and Birds

If *Archaeopteryx* really was a feathered dinosaur, then the feathers, first needed for catching insects or retaining heat, were later adapted for flying. That means dinosaurs are direct ancestors of birds.

There is a whole group of dinosaurs called ornithomimosauria (or-NITH-oh-MIME-oh-SAW-rea) or bird mimics, because they look so much like birds. The medium-sized dinosaur *Ornithomimus* (or-NITH-oh-MIME-us) has often been called an ostrich mimic. With the exception of its tail, which makes up about half of its 13-foot length, this long-necked, long-legged, swift-moving dinosaur must have

looked like a modern ostrich. *Ornithomimus* was not the direct ancestor of the ostrich, but it looked more like an ostrich than any dinosaur looked like any modern lizard.

If one branch of the dinosaurs did evolve into birds, that would mean the dinosaurs never died out completely. That one type that we now call birds not only survives, but thrives in the world today.

It's only a theory. But the thought is exciting, that the starling sitting in your backyard may number among its ancestors such giants as the mighty *Brontosaurus* and the awesome *Tyrannosaurus!*

The Death of the Dinosaurs

The dinosaurs ruled the earth for 140 million years, from the period called the Triassic to the end of the period called the Cretaceous. During that long reign some species became extinct. Others appeared for the first time.

During the Cretaceous, the stegosaurs disappeared. Many of the great saurians like the *Brontosaurus* had already died off as well. But there were still plenty of dinosaurs. Great herds of horned dinosaurs roamed what is now North America. The duck-billed dinosaurs flourished. Hunting them was that greatest of all predators, *Tyrannosaurus.*

But at the end of the Cretaceous, some sixty-five million years ago, all the dinosaurs—with the possible exception of those that had evolved into birds—were gone.

No one is sure how long it took the dinosaurs to die off. It may have happened in a week, or it could have taken a million years. But given the many millions of years of earth's history, a million years seems almost overnight.

And it wasn't just the dinosaurs that perished. The pterosaurs in the air and the plesiosaurs and other large sea dwellers also disappeared. The turtles, the frogs, and the small ancestors of the mammals survived, but many of the earth's creatures died. And no one knows why.

Was It a Meteorite?

The extinction of the dinosaurs remains one of the great mysteries of science. Some scientists believe that the earth's climate had changed at the end of the Cretaceous, and the dinosaurs had not been able to adapt. The trouble with that argument is that the earth's climate is always changing, and had changed constantly during the millions of years of dinosaurian dominance. Some dinosaurs had not been able to adapt, and they died but were replaced by other types of dinosaurs. This time the extinction was total.

Another theory is that the dinosaurs were killed by a catastrophe from space. According to this theory, sixty-five million years ago the earth was struck by a giant meteorite or asteroid. The dust from the impact would have blocked the sunlight and plunged the earth into a period of chilly darkness. Plants could not grow, and so the animals that depended on the plants for food began to die. They would be followed by the predators that ate the plant eaters. Large animals like the dinosaurs that needed a lot of food would be affected most severely by the catastrophe. After a few years the dust settled and the earth began to return to normal. But by that time it was too late for the dinosaurs.

Many scientists, however, strongly disagree with the catastrophe from space theory. It's a subject that will be argued about for a long time.

Dinosaurs Alive Today!

In recent years there have been rumors that somewhere in the swamps of Central Africa lives a large dinosaur-like creature. Perhaps you have heard such rumors.

Most scientists think the living dinosaur tales are nonsense. Still, there were a few who thought there just might be something to the stories.

Several expeditions to Central Africa were organized. The members of the expeditions fought snakes and bugs and pulled their canoes through weed-choked swamps. They heard more tales of the "dinosaur." A member of one expedition said he actually saw it at a distance and took its picture. The picture didn't come out. Expedition members examined what were supposed to be footprints. But in the end, they couldn't produce any solid evidence that this mysterious creature exists.

The chances are that it doesn't—that the great dinosaurs are indeed extinct. But we have been so fascinated by these strange and wonderful animals that we will continue to listen to rumors and hope that, somehow, one of them will turn out to be true.

Index

About the Author

Daniel Cohen is a well-known author of over one hundred books, many of them on science and related fields. Several of his works have been cited as outstanding books for children by various organizations including the Children's Book Council, the National Science Teachers Association, and the New York Public Library.

The author calls himself "a dinosaur fanatic." Though he has been interested in dinosaurs since childhood, he is particularly excited about the many major discoveries that have been made recently. Mr. Cohen resides in Port Jervis, New York, with his wife and daughter and five furry friends.

About the Artist

Jean Zallinger's award-winning illustrations have appeared in over sixty books for adults and children. Primarily a natural history artist, she has illustrated many outstanding nonfiction children's books and field guides. She has also been commissioned to illustrate for the National Wildlife Federation, *Life* magazine, Time-Life Books, Collier's Encyclopedia, and World Book Encyclopedia. Ms. Zallinger is a graduate of the Yale School of Fine Arts and currently teaches illustration at The Paier School of Art in Hamden, Connecticut.

LOCATIONS OF DINOSAUR
FOSSIL FINDS
■CRETACEOUS
▲JURASSIC
●TRIASSIC

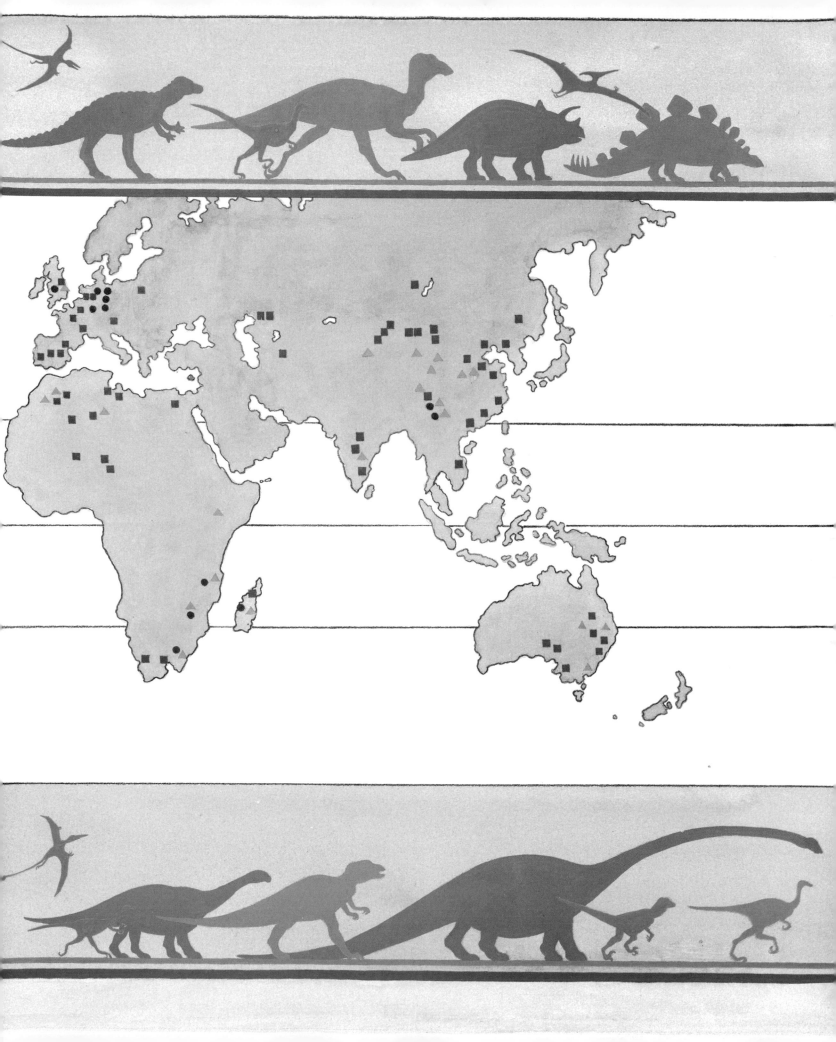